MW01234005

Breaking Boundaries?

by Russell Woods

Scythe Publications, Inc.
A Division of Winston-Derek Publishers Group, Inc.

PUBLISHED BY SCYTHE PUBLICATIONS, INC.
Nashville, Tennessee 37205

Library of Congress Catalog Card No: 92-61368
ISBN: 1-55523-560-3

Printed in the United States of America

"The greatest thing a human soul ever does in this world is to see something and tell what it saw in a plain way."
—John Ruskin

To Sue and Steve,
two of my Gods within

Cast Into Infinity

You were a part of me,
A part of my identity.
Oh, my soul you set free.
But you chose to flee,
And I ceased to be—
Cast into infinity.

Detaching you from all that I know
Is a chore I could do without.
The world's just the same,
But my mind is in doubt as to what life's about.

Baby, I've lost my way.
Time passes day after day,
And there's nothing to say.
Oh, the pain won't go away.
I do believe it's here to stay,
And my soul is beginning to fray.

I'm caught in the tide.
Taken for a ride.
With my heart open wide,
I swallow my pride.
Ooh, this feeling inside.
Where, oh where can I hide?

You tell lie after lie,
So I must say goodbye.
I let out a sigh
As I begin to cry,
And the light in my eye
Is beginning to die.

You were a part of me,
A part of my identity.
Oh, my soul you set free.
But you chose to flee,
And I ceased to be—
Cast into infinity.

Passion

I gave her my love,
And I made it crystal clear,
But I guess there are some things
That some people don't hear.

The best things in life cannot be spoken,
And the second best are misunderstood.
All lines of communication are broken.
Believe me, I'd explain it if I could.

Passion is the language I speak,
That spirit that comes from within.
My soul is aching to be received.
Oh, if you'd only just listen.

The best things are lost in translation.
My passion is taken for lust.
It's happened before, it'll happen again.
My world, it crumbles to dust.

Orgasm

Disillusioned girl
So impressed with the size.
My deepest penetration
Is done with my eyes.

Lay down for a moment.
Let me kiss your thighs.
The slightest of touch
Brings the deepest of sighs.

I'd like you to see
That the strongest of ties
Are delicately formed
On time's compromise.

One's Workground is Another's Playground

Savor each flavor
From tongue to waist.
I'm just learning to taste.

Wile in style
From shop to bar.
I just got my first car.

Shower in dower
At morn and undress.
I just acquired an address.

Embrace with grace
From uncork to close.
I'm just learning of repose.

Kiss the surface
From foot to above.
I know how to love.

Inure your contour.
Your persona befits.
But, I know my limits.

Lonely Voice of Innocence

Everywhere I look
I see anguish and despair.
Everybody's playing,
But no one's playing fair.

All I ever dream
Is to one day rise above,
And find myself a woman
Who can truly, truly love.

But the longer I search
The harder it seems.
The women I meet
Keep on shattering my dreams.

I am slowly growing numb
To this life in which we live.
We all know how to take,
But do we ever give?

I guess I'm the last
Of an ever dying breed.
My lonely voice of innocence
Echoes back with greed.

In this throw-away society
It's clear what's next is me.
I am not material,
But who will stop to see?

It's a foolish life we lead.
Where's a woman who'll agree?
I'll take her hand in mine,
And together we'll be free.

A Strand

Child, lay down your weary head.
　　The pain will not subside
　　The questions flow and collide.

Take refuge amid the insight
　　That the passage void of hope
　　Is one we all must grope.

Your suffering is not in vain.
　　It is a condition that sets you apart,
　　A true measure of your heart.

Please, let this be a strand
　　—My hand.

To Poetry

With these God-given eyes I see,
Though knowing not what next I glance,
That which reaches the core of me,
Ways of things that my life enhance.
For not this gift my guiding star,
Mislaid I'd be quite some time ago,
Lacking solace in my memoir,
Never having seen thy beauty so.

The Hush Delimits the Rush

Life is a composition.
As important as each note,
    Is the silence between.
The onerous sustains the sonorous.
The odious bounds the melodious.
The hush delimits the rush.

That is Life

To delve into the vast sea of the unknown.
To toil, to persist with courage and spirit.
To slowly make the narrowest of scopes broad.
To transform what was once infinitely complex into utter simplicity.
To explain the once unexplainable in but a few words.
To look down upon from afar the earth where you were once rooted.
That is life.

Enlightenment

Childhood is a brief interlude
    Before real life takes its grasp.
Enlightenment is the courageous struggle
    To shine despite the envelopment.

An Epiphany

I am man.
I must provide.
All these feelings
Trapped inside.

I am woman.
I must confide.
All this strength
Put aside.

Pleased to meet you.
Such a shame.
All this time not knowing
We are the same.

Unnatural

When I was a child
Nature was king.
I'd anxiously await
What each day would bring.

In the spring you'd see me
Dangling from a tree,
Embracing each limb
To find how far I could see.

In the summer I'd be
Wading through a brook,
Rearranging the rocks
To build my own little nook.

In the fall you'd find me
Wallowing in the leaves,
Piling them high
To dive with the greatest of ease.

In the winter I'd be
Sledding in the snow,
Braving the hills
To see how fast I could go.

But now I have grown,
And I find myself trapped
In a smothering routine
From which nature's detached.

At dawn you'll see me
Commuting in my car,
Not noticing the trees
As they pass from afar.

14

At noon I'll be
Toiling at my profession,
Indifferent to the seasons
As they advance their procession.

At night you'll find me
Tiring, yet awake,
Unable to fathom
The essence I forsake.

Untitleable

True love elude
    Social order claims time
Dreams be dreams
    Reality smothers
Seeds desiccate
    Apt to abort
Mind unbend
    Likely to drug
Moon remain in glory
    Ample footsteps
Page repel pen
    Wordless soul
Linger beyond reach
    Touched is lost
Flow in natural order
    Or turn to stone

To Josh

Soon be past the headache.
Just one more bottle of beer.
You don't live by the rules.

Soon be past the dry mouth.
Just one more hit of cannabis.
God just spoke to you.

Soon be past the spins.
Just one more mouthful of 'shrooms.
Have to break through the doors.

Soon be past the dry heaves.
Just one more drop of acid.
But, how do you know you won't die?

We stood at a crossroads.
You chose your way, I mine.
Who's to say who's happier?
I'll meet you on the other side.

From Josh

Soon be past the headache.
Just one more exam to ace.
Have to live by the rules.

Soon be past the patronization.
Just one more year on the job.
God is helping you.

Soon be past the liabilities.
Just one more investment to make.
Have to open the doors.

Soon be past the problems.
Just shield the kids from the pain.
But, how will they even know they're alive?

We came to a crossroads.
You chose your way, I mine.
I'll answer that question,
When I greet you on the other side.

Yet Another Maze

The mind is a curious faculty,
Inclined to labyrinthian form.
Weeks lost within each corridor,
Consumed by a single preoccupation.
Wanting, fearing, hoping, worrying,
Permeating the passageways.
Cherishing each brief liberation,
Before realizing yet another maze.

Shaded Stipulations

Education in the youthful year,
Maturate a mind that's clear.

Affinity of a colorful culture,
Nurture a heart that's pure.

Suffering along the rugged route,
Sustain a soul that's devout.

The Barren Zone

In this information age
The poor are disconnected.
The data flows overhead
Unapprehended and undetected.

Those who have good fortune
Use knowledge as their map,
While the indigent remain below,
Unable to bridge the gap.

Soon there will be a computer
In each and every home.
Just one more advancement
To expand the barren zone.

We must stop the welfare checks
That are exhausted day to day,
And found the passage of property
That will subsist to pave the way.

We must lay down our hands
And lift our brothers up,
To provide each an occasion
To drink from wisdom's cup.

Polished Product

Fallen family
Beaten body
Slight soul
Lost love
Sapped spirit
Molded mind
Void voice
Desperate dream
Circling cog
Fabricated felicity
Precious pawn
Friendly fear
Alienated American

In a Wrinkle of Time

In a wrinkle of time,
A child is conceived,
But the mother moves on,
Soon after the son is received.

The father follows his heart,
To vanquish his destiny,
And teaches his son,
To have the passion of three.

One day the father finds,
A fear that cannot be detained.
His son is no longer there,
And their love has seemingly waned.

The son's being is held,
In a wrinkle of time.
A child is conceived,
An eerie visit from the sublime.

The son follows his heart,
And postpones the gift of life.
His existence has shown him,
He must be one with a wife.

In a wrinkle of time,
As they're tumbling through,
They search for their footing,
As the future comes into view.

Looking back they're astounded,
How precariously the past has lain,
On a verge of life and death,
In a gap between joy and pain.

Somehow they're still standing,
Reunited yet worn.
One thing remains clear,
Another son must be born.

Family Gazebo

The shapely ivy tickled as it grew,
Whispering sweet nothings to the trellis,
Warmly weaving vital vines in and through,
Pleasing birds with spare berries of promise.
Ere long disease beset to take its hold,
And a neighbor's sharp shears divorced the rest.
He thought his greenhouse safer than the cold,
Leaving the gazebo sadly undressed.
Since the softwood tone has wanly withdrawn.
A few posts have fallen into small isles,
Seeking the soothing comfort of the lawn,
As others hang in fatigue from the miles.
    No ivy remains to allay the fear,
    Only posts too hardened to shed a tear.

The Equalizer

Beauty see ugliness
Sorrow grasp happiness
Wealth ogle poverty
Loneliness behold love
Age discover youth
Masculinity glimpse femininity
Adolescence ponder parenthood
Adultery spy jealousy
Minority descry majority
Bondage discern freedom

Fire level halls
Masses thrive
Haughty writhe

ConFusion

ABombination
TactiCallosity
DisarmAmentia
InabsOrbaBlemish
ApPalliDilapidation
SuburbAnnihilation
ElimiNatiOnset
GloBallistophobia

The children of Hiroshima
    have experienced the fear.
We can only fear the experience.

Freedom from the Self

I've reached that age,
When I want that which is not.
Without regard for what I have,
Without awareness, freedom is sought.

Freedom from the self.

But to continue to grow,
I make the best of what is had.
For the freedom I desire,
Is only bestowed upon the dead.

Thank You

You have shown me abuse,
Now I know not to hit.
You have shown me strife,
Now I know not to aggress.
You have shown me poverty,
Now I value money.
You have shown me failure,
Now I savor success.
You have shown me deception,
Now I know not to lie.
You have shown me pain,
Now I appreciate joy.
You have shown me hate,
Now I know how to love.

You have taught me,
And I have learned well.

A Prayer

I am early man.
My Gods are without.
I know not beyond the horizon,
Nor of the tempest about.

Sweet novelty
Amidst the open air.
Wonder widens my heart,
And encourages me to dare.

I am modern man.
My Gods are within.
I travel the globe inside a day,
With science as my beacon.

Bitter staleness
Behind my closed door.
Devices divert my mind,
And entertain me 'til I bore.

Fill me with a bit of mystery.
Give me a glimpse beyond the pall.
Bathe me in Your sweet Beauty.
Remind me that I am small.

Lost Lesson

Okay cadet Bush,
This here's a firing line.
Fifty people all in a row,
What strategy will you design?

One person may be Saddam,
Or an innocent civilian alike.
You hold the issue in your hand,
How do you plan to strike?

By Storm of course,
Blow each one away.
Shoot first, ask questions later,
Is that not the taught way?

Only in the heat of battle,
When time you cannot claim.
You are in no danger here,
And this is not a video game.

These people were all decoys,
Not one was even your foe.
Now do it again and remember,
Certain principles you never forego.

Shortcoming

Upper-class man with the upper hand,
Funny you need the underhanded.
Pilfer millions from harmless families,
Sent on vacation and unhanded.

Your assets are held,
For you to reclaim.
Take a dip in the pool,
Right back in the game.

Lower-class man with the low spirit,
Funny you think you're high-minded.
Steal bread to feed your family,
Thrown in jail and reminded.

All you have is taken,
As if you hadn't already a feat.
Putrefy in confinement,
Right back on the street.

You've got it all,
But a few pennies you lack.
Keep tightening the squeeze,
Until they can't bounce back.

Now you've got your recession,
Have to keep them at bay.
Anger enough people,
Catch a bullet someday.

America, Cocoon

Proboscis sucking nutrients,
From warm pupa, keeping dry.
Learn through semi-lucid pockets,
Yet foreign to other loci.

Infrastructure fastened appendages,
Sustained through metamorphosis.
Certain chrysalis desiccation,
Persevere or fall to paralysis.

Thorax expanding through,
As ocelli glimpse daylight.
Simply shed the integument,
Dare say ready to take flight.

Everything for Nothing

America loves a success story—
Heaven forbid it should see the
   hard work and sacrifice that
   goes into one.

I Sense I've Just Begun

I drink the insight of the intellectual.
I hear the delight of the socialite.

I breathe the endowment of the affluent.
I touch the remnant of the indigent.

I scent the purity of the infant.
I see the profundity of the elderly.

I carry no judgment,
For we are all of One,
And with each tale,
I sense I've just begun.

Happiness

Clever conversation
Simple smiles
Wandering worries
Stray sublimations
Flowing fate
Enchanting energy
Sharp senses
Lustrous lights
Crisp clime

Treasure happiness in your moon,
For it will pass forth soon.

Candlelight

I happened upon her waxen outline,
Standing rigid amid the crisp clear cold.
I struck my lone matchbook along its spine,
And cupped my hand to the west wind so bold.
My warmth climbed along her braid to her skin,
Softening her center with gentle grace,
To a treasureful pool of paraffin,
And beads of joy rolled dearly down her face.
She cast a sweet soft light into the air,
Glowing as a supple shape slowly came.
The aura held me to gaze ever there,
And still today my hand shelters her flame.
    One wee spark thankful to meet in the night,
    An unfailing return of candlelight.

Twist of Fate

Obscure origin
Many miles
Scant smiles
Unforeseen unrest
Strange surroundings
Mirroring mate
Engaging environs
Procreating peace
Seeding smiles
Many miles
Distinct destination

Why Do You Love Me?

Is it the diamond glint of wine tint,
While dining slow in candle glow?

Is it the fleeting hour of spring shower,
While sitting tied by fire side?

Is it the looking eyes of smiling guise,
While thoughts exude a gentle mood?

Is it the heart beat from body heat,
While souls meet with tangled feet?

Is it the lasting dream of shared theme,
While walking through a life anew?

Perhaps I already know.

So Much More

Sometimes I look at you
   and see beauty.
But sometimes I look at you
   and experience Beauty.

Will of Friends

You absorb the friendship I offer you,
Your body it flows through.
It filters back to me,
As pure as can be.

I absorb the friendship you offer me,
My body it flows through freely.
It filters back to you,
The feelings of one shared between two.

With that cycle flowing,
There can be nothing but learning and growing.
The will to accept another person is rare,
But that will you and I share.

Many are unable to see,
How special a friendship can be.
They fear what they do not know,
And are unable to grow.

We see in each other the will to be kind,
That is so often hard to find.
A chance we are willing to take,
So a friendship we can make.

What is plain for us to see,
Is friends we are willing to be.
And with that will we are not blind,
And growth between us we will find.

Inspiration

Your strength gives me focus,
As shards of weakness pattern twilight.
Your beauty is my handhold,
As gales of despair menace my upright.

Your truth is my foothold,
As bits of lies dislodge and plummet.
Your patience is my protection,
As clouds of precipitance converge the summit.

Your being is my distinction,
As moments of exhaustion ease my pace.
Your love is my compassion,
As hands of others adopt my place.

An Alternative

I've been blessed with the chance
To spend a week on a boat.
I dare say there is no equal
To keep my dreams afloat.

The sun on my skin,
The wind in my hair,
The salt in my mouth,
Jimmy Buffett in the air.

The day's catch on the grill,
The sound of the tide,
The moon and stars up above,
My girl by my side.

Intimate with nature that provides
Everything I need to survive.
Far from civilization that averts
My soul from coming alive.

In a Word

You have a word for us.
Dysfunctional.
Sum families up in a word.
Aren't they absurd?

We can play that game, too.
Dysfunctional.
Sum governments up in a word.
Yes, you are absurd.

I am truly grateful,
For the opportunities I own.
But I am a rarity,
A life that managed to atone.

I ask for your truth,
In compassion for the plight.
But who am I,
To ask for what is Right?

I believe in America,
And the American way.
You have earned your riches,
And I will join you someday.

But we must pioneer,
A minimum life for all.
A house that is a home.
An education to stand tall.

Not violence infested schools,
And drug infested slums.
They have no money or spirit,
Only despair that misbecomes.

Decent single-family homes,
In neighborhoods that are well-kept.
And well-funded schools,
With teachers that accept.

Perhaps you've not witnessed the struggle,
So that I cannot adduce.
But I am telling you of it,
And now you have no excuse.

A minor redistribution of wealth,
To give all a minimum chance.
Not much to ask America,
A country of such great stance.

So I break through the boundary,
And refuse to sum you up in a word.
Do you step through to greet me?
Or are we both absurd?

A New Day

I dive to the sea.
The water gathers,
To cleanse my darkness
As it lathers.

I rise to the sky.
The sun rushes,
To melt my coldness
As it blushes.